Stations of the
Infant
Jesus

Stations of the
Infant Jesus

St Alphonsus Liguori

Published by Redemptorist Publications

Wolf's Lane, Chawton, Hampshire, GU34 3HQ, UK
Tel. +44 (0)1420 88222, Fax. +44 (0)1420 88805
Email: rp@rpbooks.co.uk, www.rpbooks.co.uk

A registered charity limited by guarantee
Registered in England 03261721
Copyright © Redemptorist Publications 2019

First published December 2019
Edited by Denis McBride C.Ss.R. and Giselle Nizinskyj-Beaumont
Designed by Laura Gatie

ISBN 978-0-85231-565-1

All rights reserved. No part of this publication may be reproduced, stored in a retrieval system, or transmitted in any form or by any means, electronic, mechanical, photocopying, recording or otherwise, without prior permission in writing from Redemptorist Publications.
A CIP catalogue record for this book is available from the British Library

The publisher gratefully acknowledges permission to use the following copyright material:

Excerpts from The Jerusalem Bible, copyright © 1966 by Darton, Longman & Todd, Ltd and Doubleday, a division of Random House, Inc. Reprinted by permission.

Excerpts from the New Revised Standard Version of the Bible: Anglicised Edition, © 1989. 1995, Division of Christian Education of the National Council of the Churches of Christ in the United States of America. Used by permission. All rights reserved.

Redemptorist Publications are grateful to the Redemptorist General Council in Rome for permission to use the official photo of the restored icon of Our Lady of Perpetual Succour in the church of St Alphonsus, Via Merulana 26, Rome.

Printed by Elanders UK Ltd.

INTRODUCTION

Two saintly men, untethered in history, believed the same thing: that the most distinguishing belief of the Catholic Church was not the resurrection but the incarnation – that the Son of the almighty God had become fully human, that the Word that was at home in God pitched his tent among us and made a new home, as the son of Mary of Nazareth, in the world of first-century Palestine. Divine majesty not only looked down, but came down to make his home among us. He was the stranger from heaven, unrecognised by his creation, unacknowledged by his own people. Hosanna, now, not in the highest but in the lowest. The two great advocates of this fundamental characteristic of Catholic belief were St Alphonsus Liguori, the founder of the Redemptorists, and St John Henry Newman, the distinguished Oratorian and theologian.

Their celebration of the incarnation was not a holy memory of an astounding event that happened two thousand years ago, but a profound appreciation of the ongoing presence of Christ in word and in sacrament and in the midst of everyday life. Jesus is among us today.

In writing my own *Stations of the Infancy* it was unavoidable that I would revisit and reflect upon the original *Stations of the Infant Jesus* written by St Alphonsus, a Doctor of the Church. St Alphonsus was the writer, nay composer, of many reflections, prayers and books – 111 in total – all with the declared intent of helping readers draw closer to the heart of God whilst offering his own heartfelt devotion to his Saviour. His *Stations of the Cross* and *Visits to the Blessed Sacrament* remain popular and enduring classics: indeed Redemptorist Publications publishes beautiful editions of both. St Alphonsus' *Stations of the Infant Jesus* until this new edition was out of print. It is my hope that this elegant version, with beautiful illustrations by Laura Gatie, will propel it back into the Catholic Advent canon where its absence should have been rectified long before now.

Reading St Alphonsus' *Stations of the Infant Jesus* is like overhearing a loving and attentive grandfather whisper tender assurances into the cradle in the quiet of the night. His conversational intimacy and his muscular sentimentality might appear strange in a world of propriety that edges towards detachment. You feel privileged, if somewhat uneasy, to witness such overflowing devotion. You wonder about how both are so tethered together.

I hope you enjoy journeying through the Gospel beginnings of the Jesus story, celebrating the astounding truth that God came among us in Christ at a particular time and place in history, but never forgetting that Christ comes to us every day in word and sacrament and people.

Denis McBride C.Ss.R.
Publishing Director

STATION I
The Son of God becomes an Infant

Opening Prayer

V. Incline unto my aid, O God.
R. O Lord, make haste to help me.
Glory be to the Father, etc.

◆

O Jesus, born of Virgin bright,
Immortal glory be to thee;
Praise to the Father infinite,
And Holy Ghost eternally.

Consideration

Consider that the Son of God, the Infinite Majesty, the Creator of the world, and who has need of no one, became incarnate to save a lost man by his sufferings, and was for nine months enclosed as a little infant in the most chaste womb of Mary.

Affections

O most amiable Infant Jesus, God and Man, it was thy burning love for me which urged thee do all this. I give thee thanks; and beseech thee, by thy Incarnation, to give me the grace to correspond to such great goodness.

O my sweetest Love, I am sorry that I have offended thee. I desire to be always faithful in thy service: enkindle in me thy love; make me chaste and holy.

O Mary, grant that I may belong entirely to thee and to thy Son Jesus.

Hail Mary, etc. Glory be to the Father, etc.

Closing Responses

V. Blessed is the womb of the Virgin Mary,
   which bore the Son of the eternal Father.
R. And blessed are the breasts which gave
   suck to Christ our Lord.

◆

O Jesus, ever sweetest Lord,
And ever loving still;
From this dear crib sweet drops of love
Into my heart distil.

STATION II
Jesus is born an Infant

Opening Prayer

V. Incline unto my aid, O God.
R. O Lord, make haste to help me.
Glory be to the Father, etc.

O Jesus, born of Virgin bright,
Immortal glory be to thee;
Praise to the Father infinite,
And Holy Ghost eternally.

Consideration

Consider that Jesus at his birth has not even a wretched cabin, such as the poorest have; but is born in a cold cavern, and is laid in a manger upon straw.

Affections

O most holy Infant Jesus, I thank thee for this; and I beseech thee, by thy most poor and bitter birth, grant that I may reap the fruits of thy coming on this earth.

O my sweetest Love, I am sorry that I have offended thee. I desire to be always faithful in thy service: enkindle in me thy love; make me chaste and holy.

O Mary, grant that I may belong entirely to thee and to thy Son Jesus.

Hail Mary, etc. Glory be to the Father, etc.

Closing responses

V. Blessed is the womb of the Virgin Mary,
which bore the Son of the Eternal Father.
R. And blessed are the breasts which gave
suck to Christ our Lord.

◆

O Jesus, ever sweetest Lord,
And ever loving still;
From this dear crib sweet drops of love
Into my heart distil.

STATION III
Jesus is suckled

Opening Prayer

V. Incline unto my aid, O God.
R. O Lord, make haste to help me.
Glory be to the Father, etc.

◆

O Jesus, born of Virgin bright,
Immortal glory be to thee;
Praise to the Father infinite,
And Holy Ghost eternally.

Consideration

Consider that God, Majesty itself, who gives food to men and beasts, is born an Infant, and has recourse to Mary for his food; and he, through whom not a sparrow hungers, is fed with a little milk.

Affections

O most lovely Infant, thou takest milk, to be changed into that flesh which one day is to be bruised and torn for me. I thank thee for this goodness; and I beseech thee by this purest milk, grant me grace to act always with a pure intention of pleasing thee, even as thou didst ever act with the sole aim of obtaining my eternal happiness.

O my sweetest Love, I am sorry that I have offended thee. I desire to be always faithful in thy service: enkindle in me thy love; make me chaste and holy.

O Mary, grant that I may belong entirely to thee and to thy Son Jesus.

Hail Mary, etc. Glory be to the Father, etc.

Closing responses

V. Blessed is the womb of the Virgin Mary,
which bore the Son of the Eternal Father.
R. And blessed are the breasts which gave
suck to Christ our Lord.

◆

O Jesus, ever sweetest Lord,
And ever loving still;
From this dear crib sweet drops of love
Into my heart distil.

STATION IV
Jesus is wrapped in swaddling clothes

Opening Prayer

V. Incline unto my aid, O God.
R. O Lord, make haste to help me.
Glory be to the Father, etc.

◆

O Jesus, born of Virgin bright,
Immortal glory be to thee;
Praise to the Father infinite,
And Holy Ghost eternally.

Consideration

Consider that the Infinite God, whom the heavens cannot contain, made an Infant for us, vouchsafed to be wrapped by Mary in swaddling clothes, and covered with poor rags. And thus the hands and feet of God by swathing bands are tied.

Affections

O gentlest Infant, thou art tied in swathing bands to deliver my soul from the chains of sin and hell. I thank thee; grant, by thy holy humility, that, casting away every other bond, I may live bound and united to thee.

O my sweetest Love, I am sorry that I have offended thee. I desire to be always faithful in thy service: enkindle in me thy love; make me chaste and holy.

O Mary, grant that I may belong entirely to thee and to thy Son Jesus.

Hail Mary, etc. Glory be to the Father, etc.

Closing responses

V. Blessed is the womb of the Virgin Mary,
which bore the Son of the Eternal Father.
R. And blessed are the breasts which gave
suck to Christ our Lord.

◆

O Jesus, ever sweetest Lord,
And ever loving still;
From this dear crib sweet drops of love
Into my heart distil.

STATION V
Jesus is circumcised

Opening Prayer
V. Incline unto my aid, O God.
R. O Lord, make haste to help me.
Glory be to the Father, etc.

◆

O Jesus, born of Virgin bright,
Immortal glory be to thee;
Praise to the Father infinite,
And Holy Ghost eternally.

Consideration
Consider that the Infant Jesus, eight days after his birth, showed himself to be even then our Saviour, by shedding for us his divine blood in the circumcision.

Affections

O most merciful Infant God, I give thee thanks; and I beseech thee, by the pain which thou didst feel, and by the blood which thou didst shed in thy circumcision, grant me grace and power to pluck out of my heart, and to cast from it, all earthly affections.

O my sweetest Love, I am sorry that I have offended thee. I desire to be always faithful in thy service: enkindle in me thy love; make me chaste and holy.

O Mary, grant that I may belong entirely to thee and to thy Son Jesus.

Hail Mary, etc. Glory be to the Father, etc.

Closing responses

V. Blessed is the womb of the Virgin Mary, which bore the Son of the Eternal Father.
R. And blessed are the breasts which gave suck to Christ our Lord.

◆

O Jesus, ever sweetest Lord,
And ever loving still;
From this dear crib sweet drops of love
Into my heart distil.

STATION VI
Jesus is adored by the Magi

Opening Prayer

V. Incline unto my aid, O God.
R. O Lord, make haste to help me.
Glory be to the Father, etc.

O Jesus, born of Virgin bright,
Immortal glory be to thee;
Praise to the Father infinite,
And Holy Ghost eternally.

Consideration

Consider that the Infant God is visited and adored by the Magi, who, though Gentiles, were enlightened by faith to acknowledge this Man-God for their Saviour, and offered him gold, frankincense and myrrh.

Affections

Most adorable Redeemer, I too have received from thee this great gift of faith. I thank thee for it; and I beseech thee, by the glory of this thy manifestation, grant that, like the Magi, I may correspond and be faithful to thy grace.

O my sweetest Love, I am sorry that I have offended thee. I desire to be always faithful in thy service: enkindle in me thy love; make me chaste and holy.

O Mary, grant that I may belong entirely to thee and to thy Son Jesus.

Hail Mary, etc. Glory be to the Father, etc.

Closing responses

V. Blessed is the womb of the Virgin Mary,
which bore the Son of the Eternal Father.
R. And blessed are the breasts which gave
suck to Christ our Lord.

◆

O Jesus, ever sweetest Lord,
And ever loving still;
From this dear crib sweet drops of love
Into my heart distil.

STATION VII
Jesus is presented in the Temple

Opening Prayer

V. Incline unto my aid, O God.
R. O Lord, make haste to help me.
Glory be to the Father, etc.

◆

O Jesus, born of Virgin bright,
Immortal glory be to thee;
Praise to the Father infinite,
And Holy Ghost eternally.

Consideration

Consider that the Virgin Mary, forty days after the birth of the Infant Jesus, carries him in her arms to the Temple, and, offering him to God for us, consents that by his Passion and death he should become our Redeemer.

Affections

O most loving Infant, for this one end didst thou deliver thyself up to death, to bestow on me eternal life. I give thee thanks, and pray thee, by this offering of thyself, to make me constantly ready to mortify and die to myself for the love of thee.

O my sweetest Love, I am sorry that I have offended thee. I desire to be always faithful in thy service: enkindle in me thy love; make me chaste and holy.

O Mary, grant that I may belong entirely to thee and to thy Son Jesus.

Hail Mary, etc. Glory be to the Father, etc.

Closing responses

V. Blessed is the womb of the Virgin Mary,
    which bore the Son of the Eternal Father.
R. And blessed are the breasts which gave
    suck to Christ our Lord.

◆

O Jesus, ever sweetest Lord,
And ever loving still;
From this dear crib sweet drops of love
Into my heart distil.

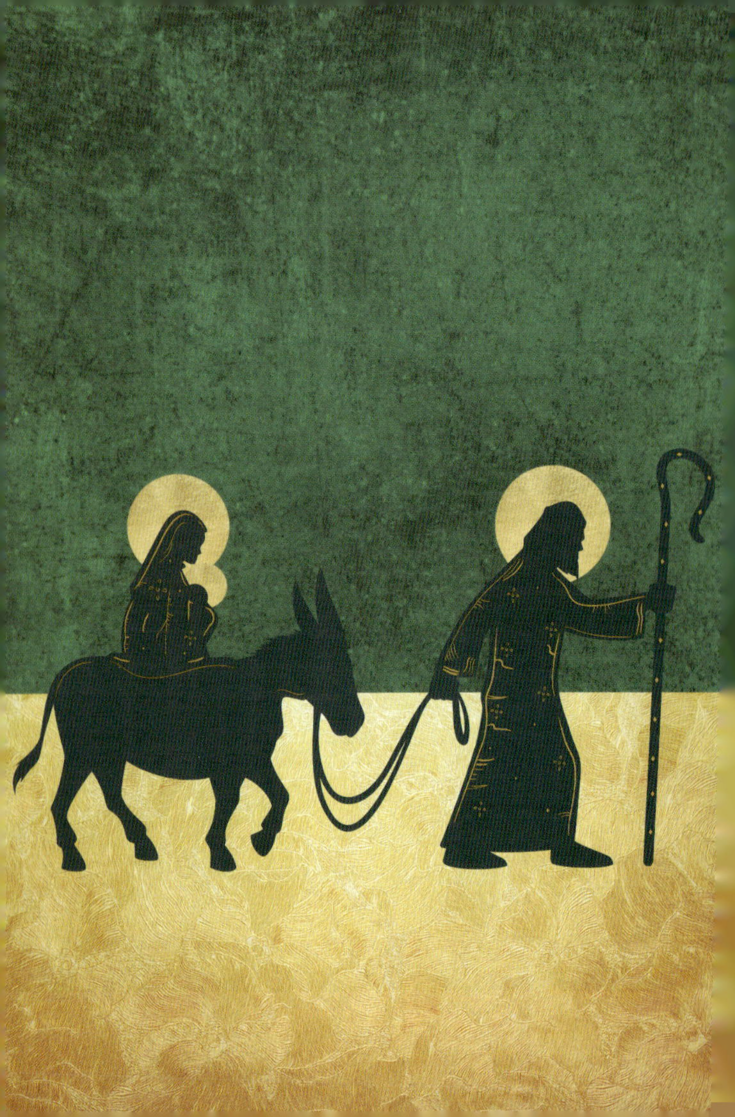

STATION VIII
Jesus flees into Egypt

Opening Prayer

V. Incline unto my aid, O God.
R. O Lord, make haste to help me.
Glory be to the Father, etc.

◆

O Jesus, born of Virgin bright,
Immortal glory be to thee;
Praise to the Father infinite,
And Holy Ghost eternally.

Consideration

Consider that Herod, fearing that Jesus would deprive him of his kingdom, plans his death; and therefore orders all the children of Bethlehem to be murdered. The most blessed Virgin, warned by an angel, takes the Infant Jesus into Egypt.

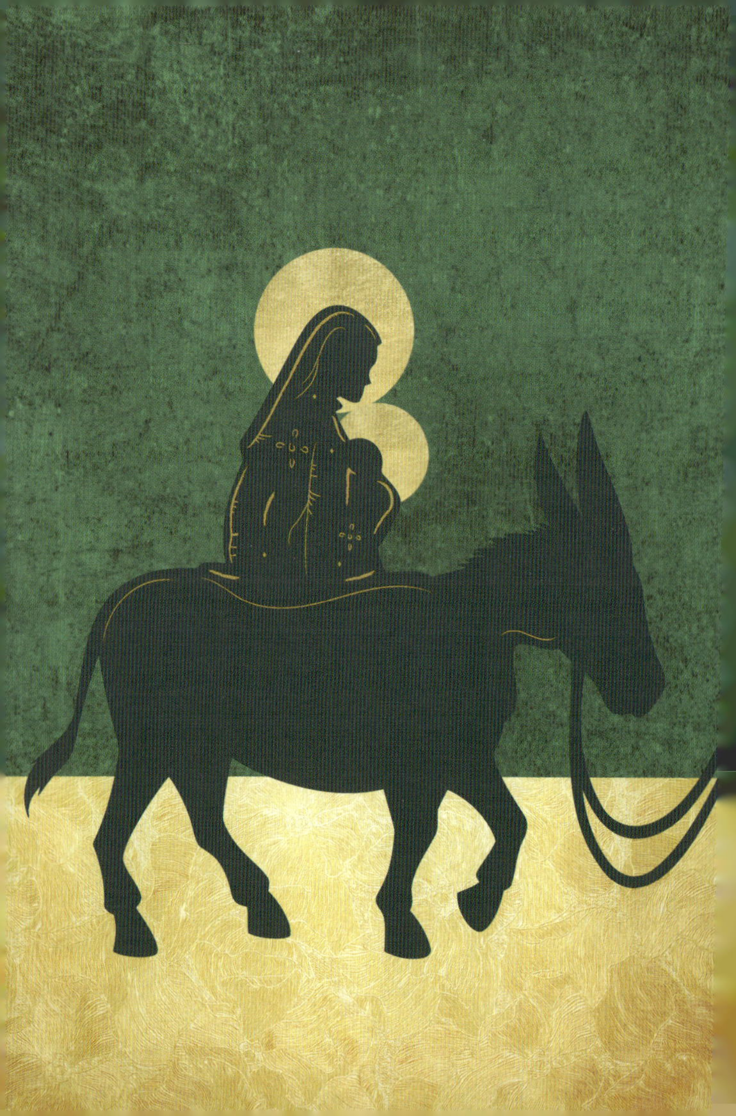

Affections

O dearest Infant, what sufferings didst thou not endure during this journey of a whole month and even longer, and that too in the depth of winter! How often wert thou drenched with rain and stiffened with the cold! How many nights didst thou pass in the open air!

I thank thee; and beseech thee by thy flight to give me strength to avoid all the dangers of eternal death.

O my sweetest Love, I am sorry that I have offended thee. I desire to be always faithful in thy service: enkindle in me thy love; make me chaste and holy.

O Mary, grant that I may belong entirely to thee and to thy Son Jesus.

Hail Mary, etc. Glory be to the Father, etc.

Closing responses

V. Blessed is the womb of the Virgin Mary,
which bore the Son of the Eternal Father.
R. And blessed are the breasts which gave
suck to Christ our Lord.

◆

O Jesus, ever sweetest Lord,
And ever loving still;
From this dear crib sweet drops of love
Into my heart distil.

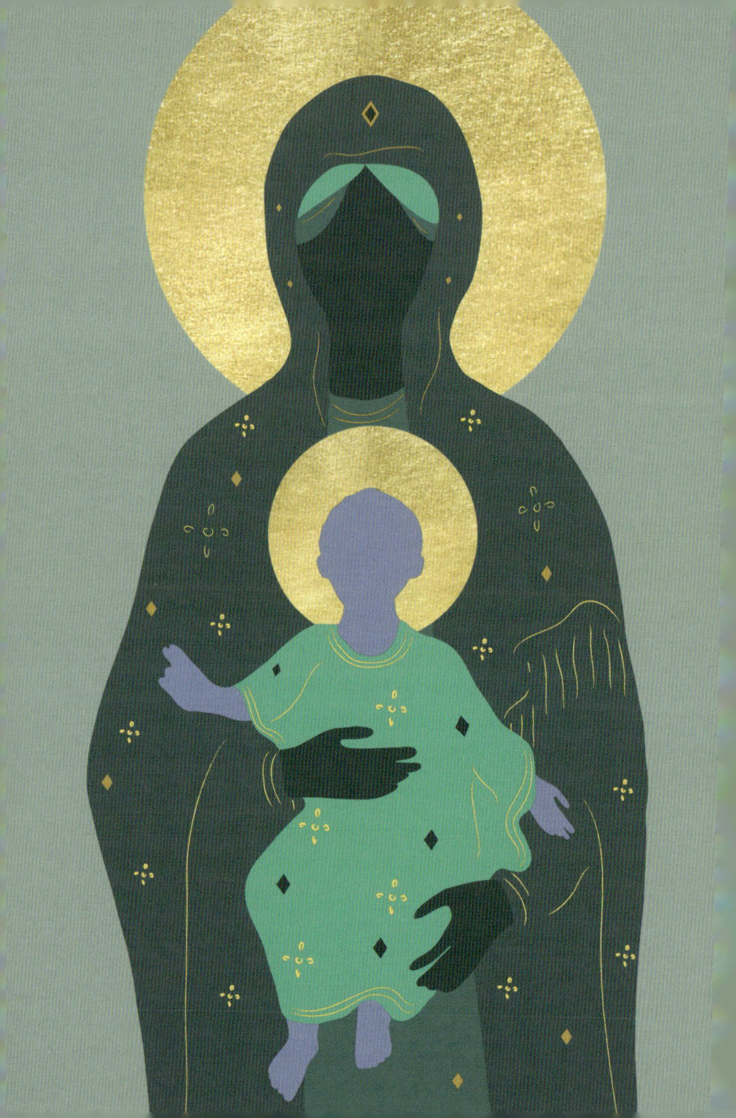

STATION IX
Jesus with his hands freed from the swaddling clothes

Opening Prayer
V. Incline unto my aid, O God.
R. O Lord, make haste to help me.
Glory be to the Father, etc.

◆

O Jesus, born of Virgin bright,
Immortal glory be to thee;
Praise to the Father infinite,
And Holy Ghost eternally.

Consideration

Consider that the Infant Jesus, some months after his birth, is still swathed by the blessed Virgin, though his hands are freed from the swaddling clothes.

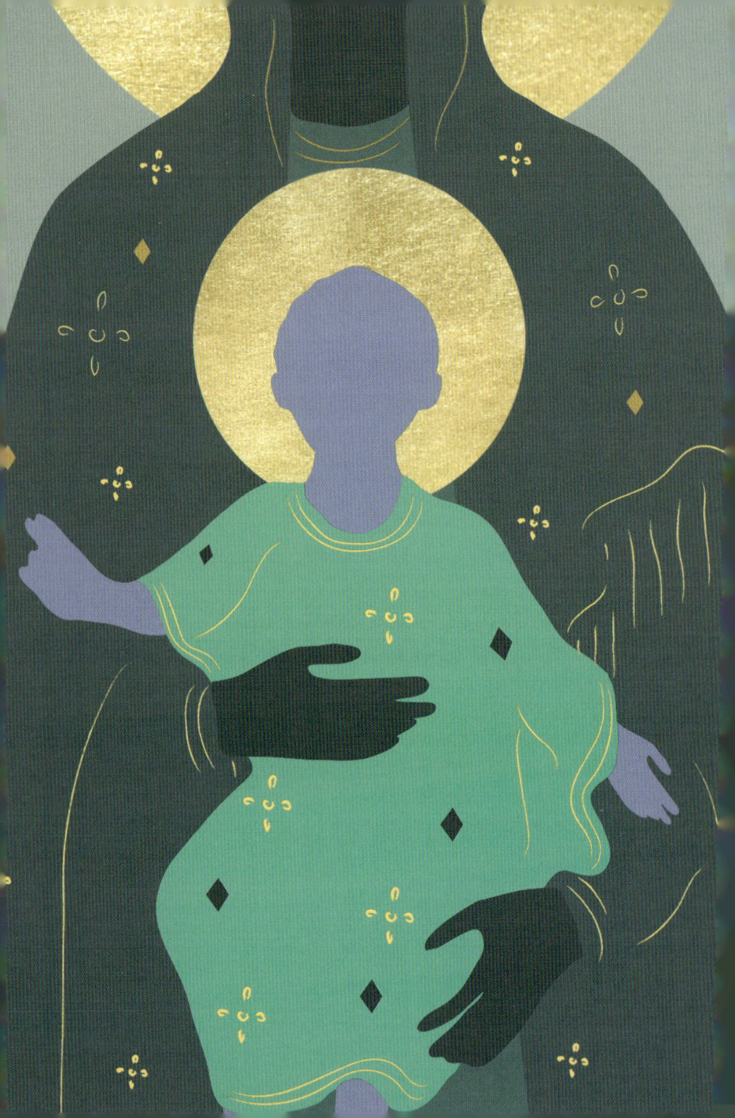

Affections

Most tender Infant, I imagine to myself that first moment when thou didst join thy little hands, and, lifting up thy divine eyes to heaven, didst intercede with the eternal Father in my behalf. I give thee thanks; and beseech thee to grant by the merits of thy prayer that my prayers may be always pleasing and acceptable in thy sight.

O my sweetest Love, I am sorry that I have offended thee. I desire to be always faithful in thy service: enkindle in me thy love; make me chaste and holy.

O Mary, grant that I may belong entirely to thee and to thy Son Jesus.

Hail Mary, etc. Glory be to the Father, etc.

Closing responses

V. Blessed is the womb of the Virgin Mary,
   which bore the Son of the Eternal Father.
R. And blessed are the breasts which gave
   suck to Christ our Lord.

◆

O Jesus, ever sweetest Lord,
And ever loving still;
From this dear crib sweet drops of love
Into my heart distil.

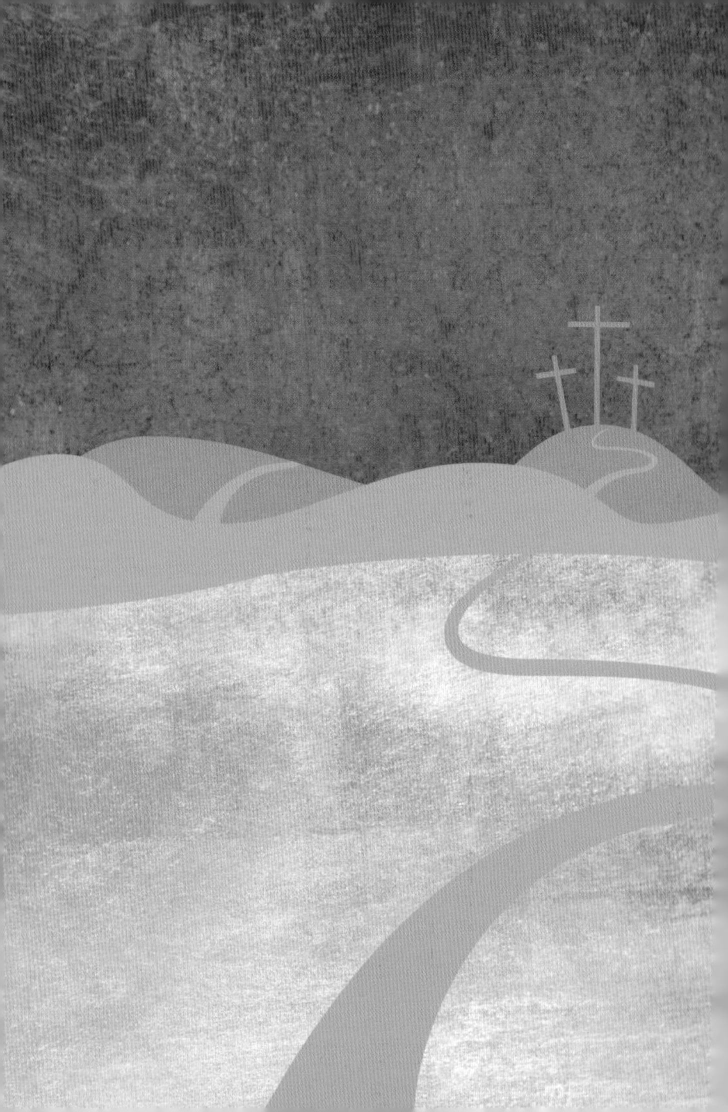

STATION X
Jesus begins to walk

Opening Prayer

V. Incline unto my aid, O God.
R. O Lord, make haste to help me.
Glory be to the Father, etc.

◆

O Jesus, born of Virgin bright,
Immortal glory be to thee;
Praise to the Father infinite,
And Holy Ghost eternally.

Consideration

Consider that the Infant Jesus, now a little older, begins to walk, and plans out in his mind the journeys he would make in the surrounding country of Judaea to preach by his most holy words the way of salvation; and at the same time figures to himself the road to Calvary, which he would tread in going to die for us.

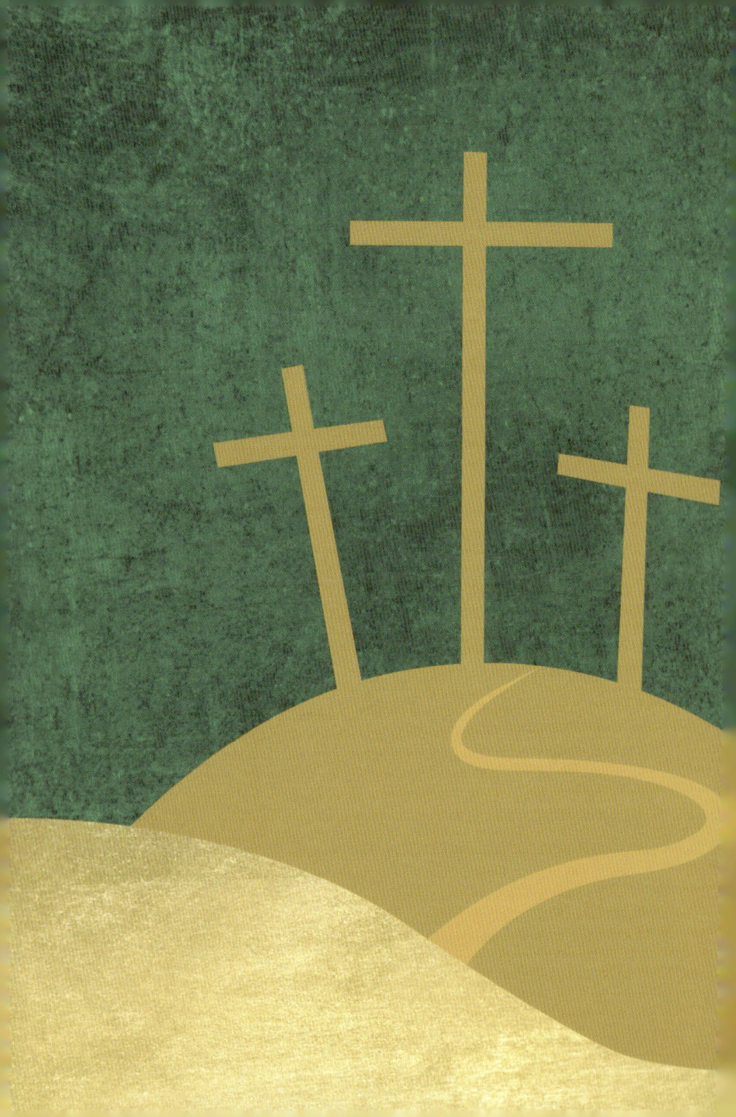

Affections

O most loving Infant, I thank thee; and beseech thee by thy first steps, grant me grace always to walk in the way which thou hast pointed out to me.

O my sweetest Love, I am sorry that I have offended thee. I desire to be always faithful in thy service: enkindle in me thy love; make me chaste and holy.

O Mary, grant that I may belong entirely to thee and to thy Son Jesus.

Hail Mary, etc. Glory be to the Father, etc.

Closing responses

V. Blessed is the womb of the Virgin Mary,
which bore the Son of the Eternal Father.
R. And blessed are the breasts which gave
suck to Christ our Lord.

◆

O Jesus, ever sweetest Lord,
And ever loving still;
From this dear crib sweet drops of love
Into my heart distil.

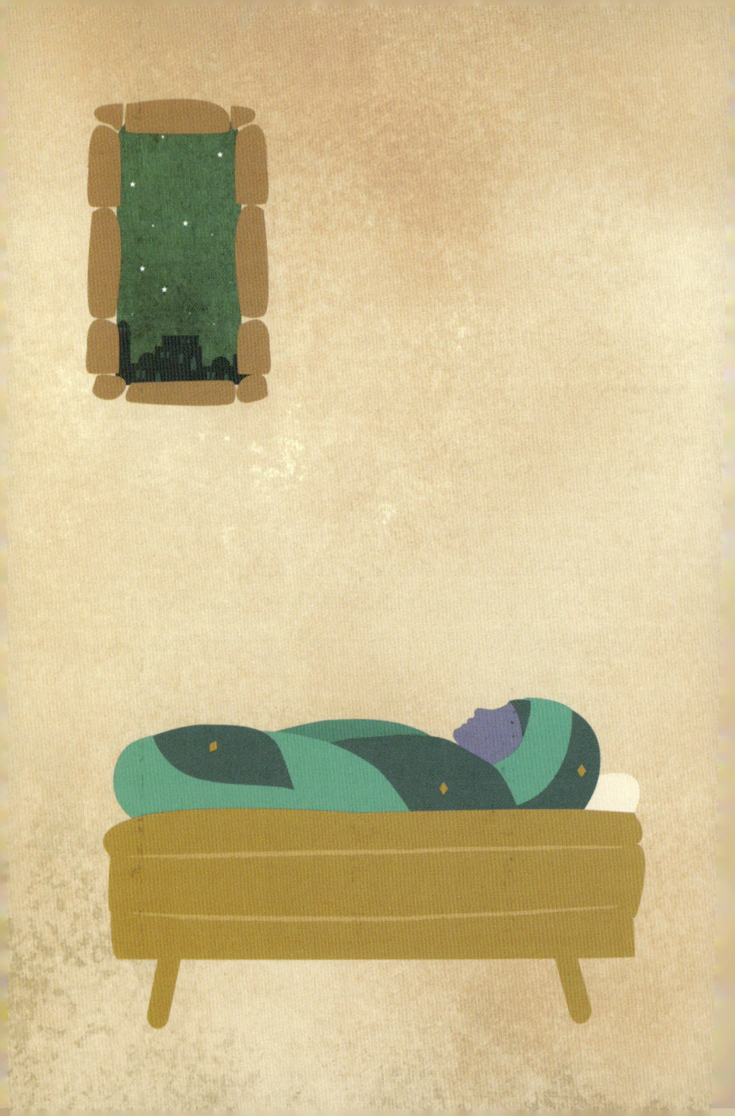

STATION XI
Jesus sleeps

Opening Prayer

V. Incline unto my aid, O God.
R. O Lord, make haste to help me.
Glory be to the Father, etc.

◆

O Jesus, born of Virgin bright,
Immortal glory be to thee;
Praise to the Father infinite,
And Holy Ghost eternally.

Consideration

Consider that the Infant Jesus lies in a poor cradle in the little house of his mother Mary, and takes his rest; and often times the bare ground serves him as a bed.

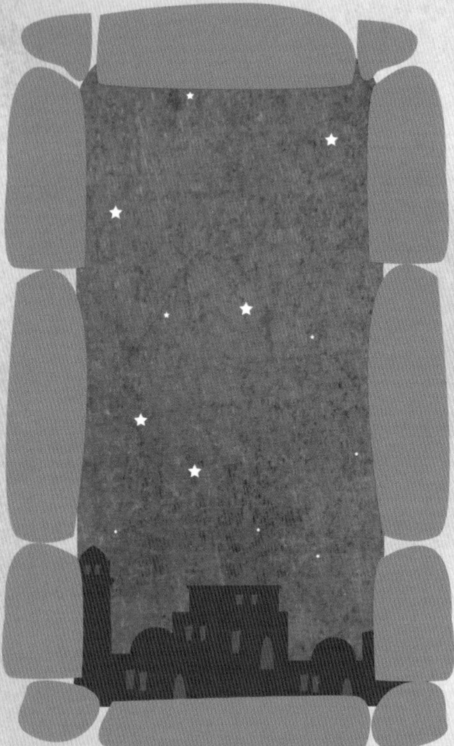

Affections

O most amiable Infant, even while sleeping thy heart watches, and thou wert loving me, and thinking upon me; and thy heart was consoled with the good which thou hadst bestowed, and would bestow, upon me. I thank thee; and pray thee, by thy loving slumbers, to give me grace to live for ever in loving thee, who art the most loving God.

O my sweetest Love, I am sorry that I have offended thee. I desire to be always faithful in thy service: enkindle in me thy love; make me chaste and holy.

O Mary, grant that I may belong entirely to thee and to thy Son Jesus.

Hail Mary, etc. Glory be to the Father, etc.

Closing responses

V. Blessed is the womb of the Virgin Mary, which bore the Son of the Eternal Father.
R. And blessed are the breasts which gave suck to Christ our Lord.

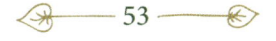

◆

O Jesus, ever sweetest Lord,
And ever loving still;
From this dear crib sweet drops of love
Into my heart distil.

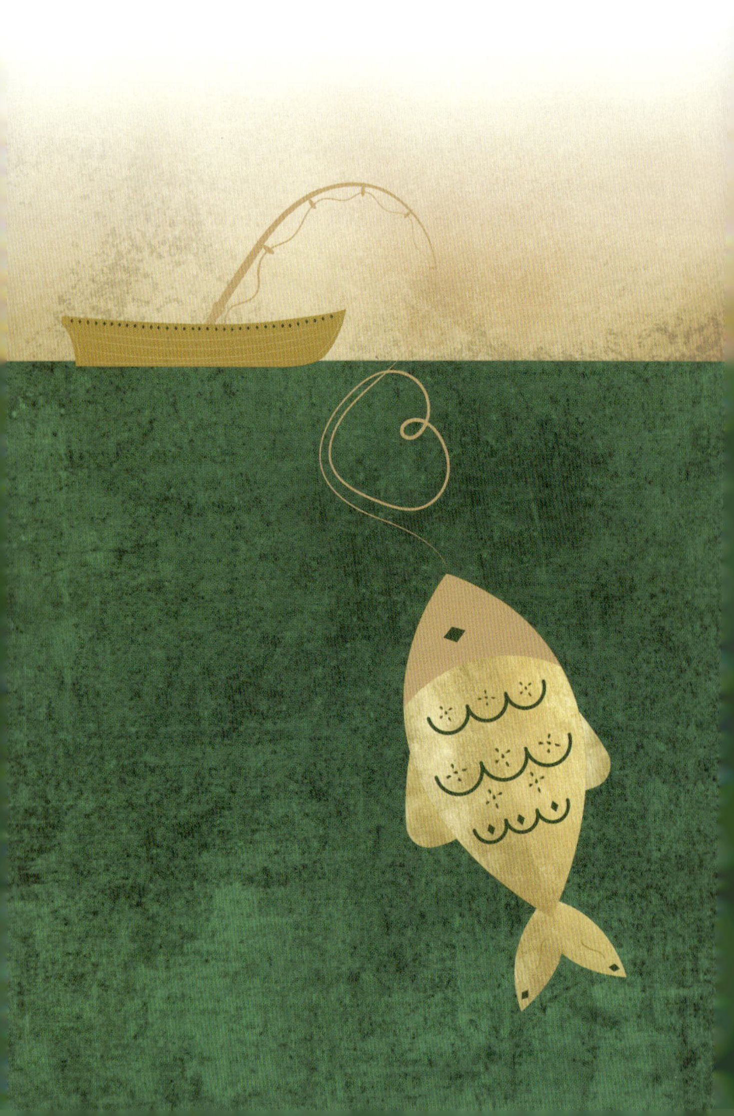

STATION XII
Jesus in the form of a fisher

Opening Prayer

V. Incline unto my aid, O God.
R. O Lord, make haste to help me.
Glory be to the Father, etc.

◆

O Jesus, born of Virgin bright,
Immortal glory be to thee;
Praise to the Father infinite,
And Holy Ghost eternally.

Consideration

Consider to yourself the Infant Jesus represented in the form of a fisher, holding in his hands a rod, to which is attached the hook where with he will catch the hearts of men. When we think on his beauty, and on the love with which he seeks us, and on all that he has done to allure us to his love, we must consecrate our hearts to his service.

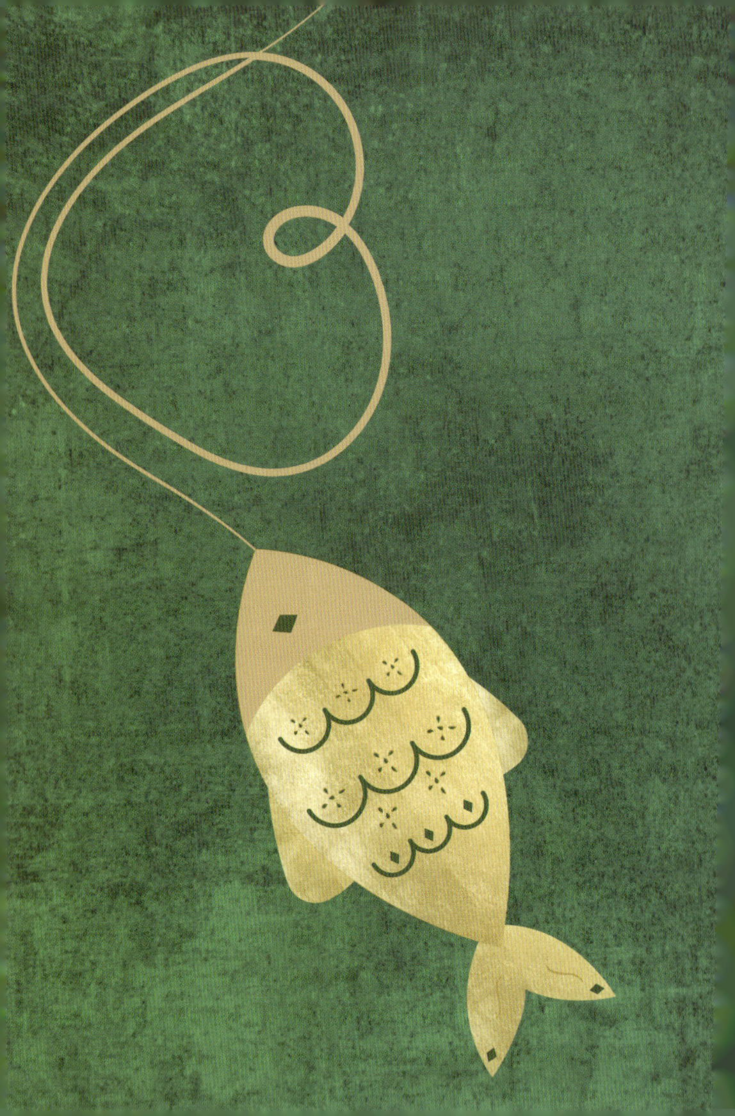

Affections

O Divine Infant, I give thee thanks; and pray thee by the zeal which thou hast shown in endeavouring to draw my heart to thee, give me the grace never to leave thee more, and grant that, having continual recourse to thee, I may become one with thee and never separate myself from thee again.

O my sweetest Love, I am sorry that I have offended thee. I desire to be always faithful in thy service: enkindle in me thy love; make me chaste and holy.

O Mary, grant that I may belong entirely to thee and to thy Son Jesus.

Hail Mary, etc. Glory be to the Father, etc.

Closing responses

V. Blessed is the womb of the Virgin Mary,
which bore the Son of the Eternal Father.
R. And blessed are the breasts which gave
suck to Christ our Lord.

◆

O Jesus, ever sweetest Lord,
And ever loving still;
From this dear crib sweet drops of love
Into my heart distil.

FINAL PRAYER

I offer and present unto thee, O most sweet Infant Jesus, the steps which I have made to venerate the mysteries of thy infancy, and the homage which I have paid thee.

I pray thee graciously to accept it, and to reward me with the virtues of childhood – chastity, humility and simplicity.

It is a joy and consolation to me when I behold thee on the altar, surrounded with so many and so lovely flowers. I ardently desire and wish to see my heart in like manner adorned with the flowers of all holy virtues, that thou mayest find thy pleasure, and dwell in it; and may it be my lot to live in this world ever united to thee, that, one with thee, I may dwell in thy presence in heaven for all eternity. Amen.

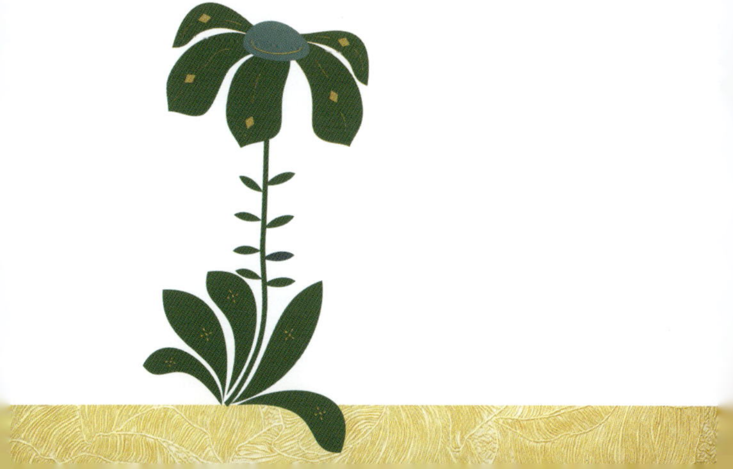